The Coloring Studio

Amazing Animals

Faratiana Andriamanga

Little, Brown and Company
New York Boston

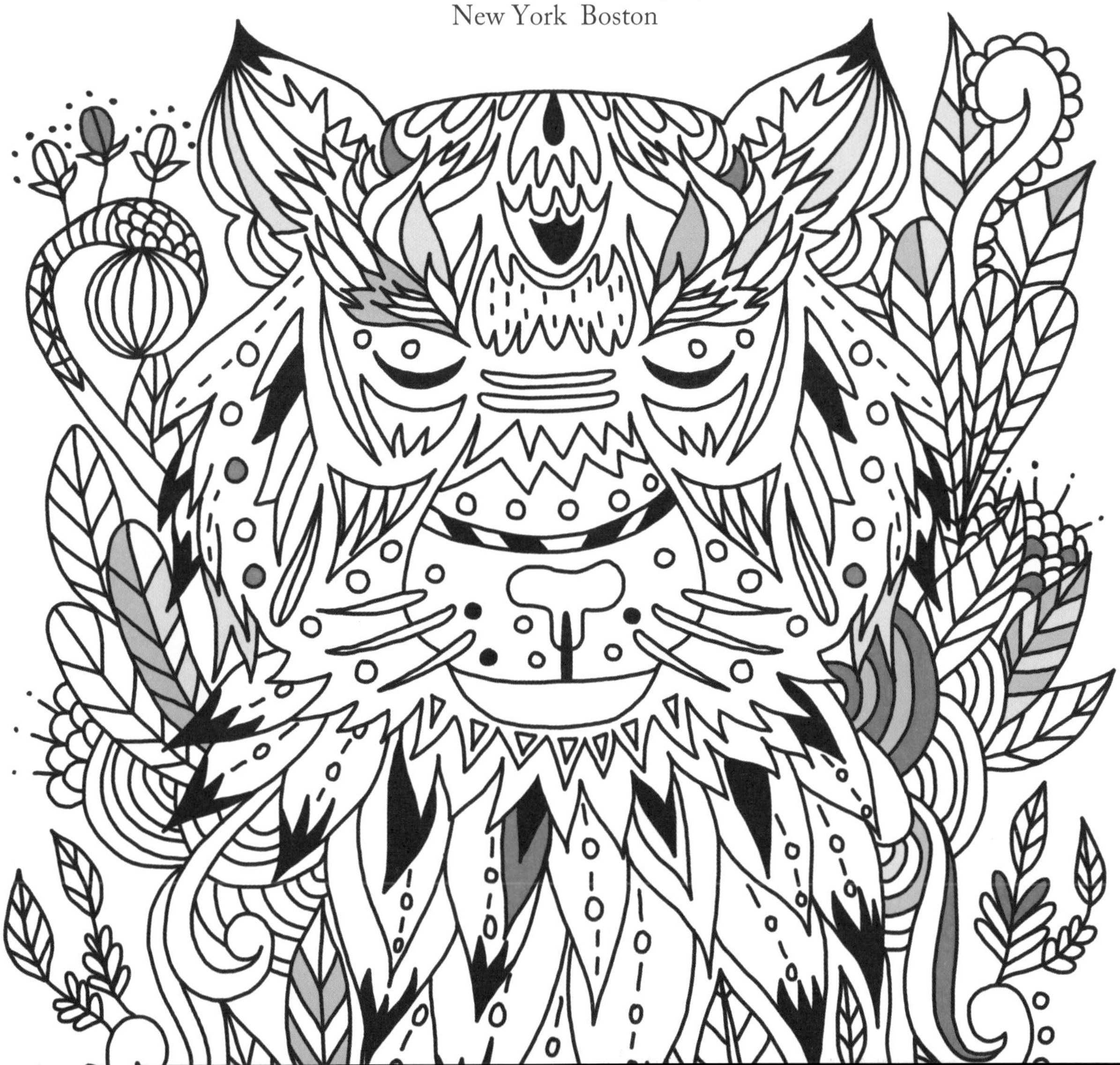

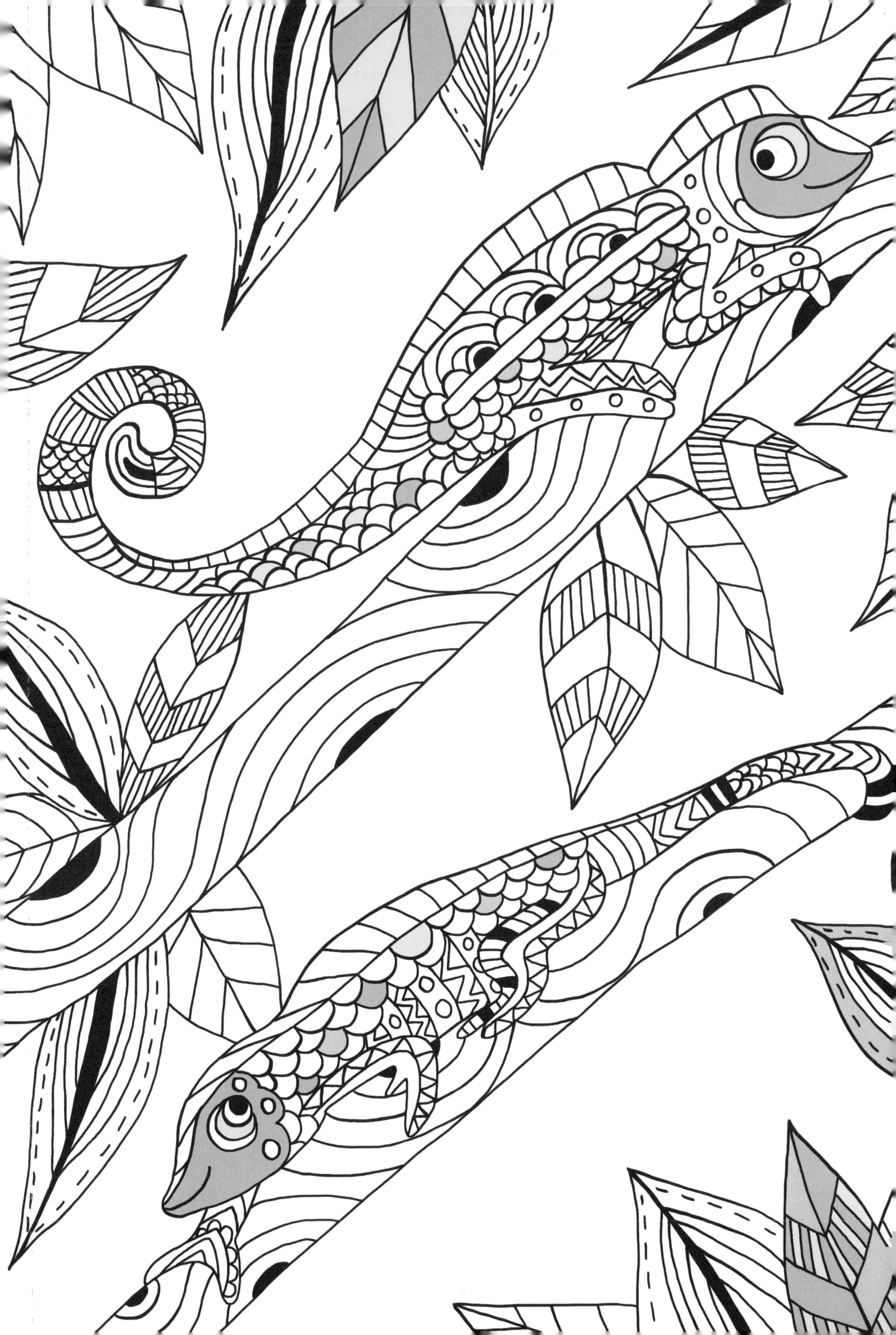

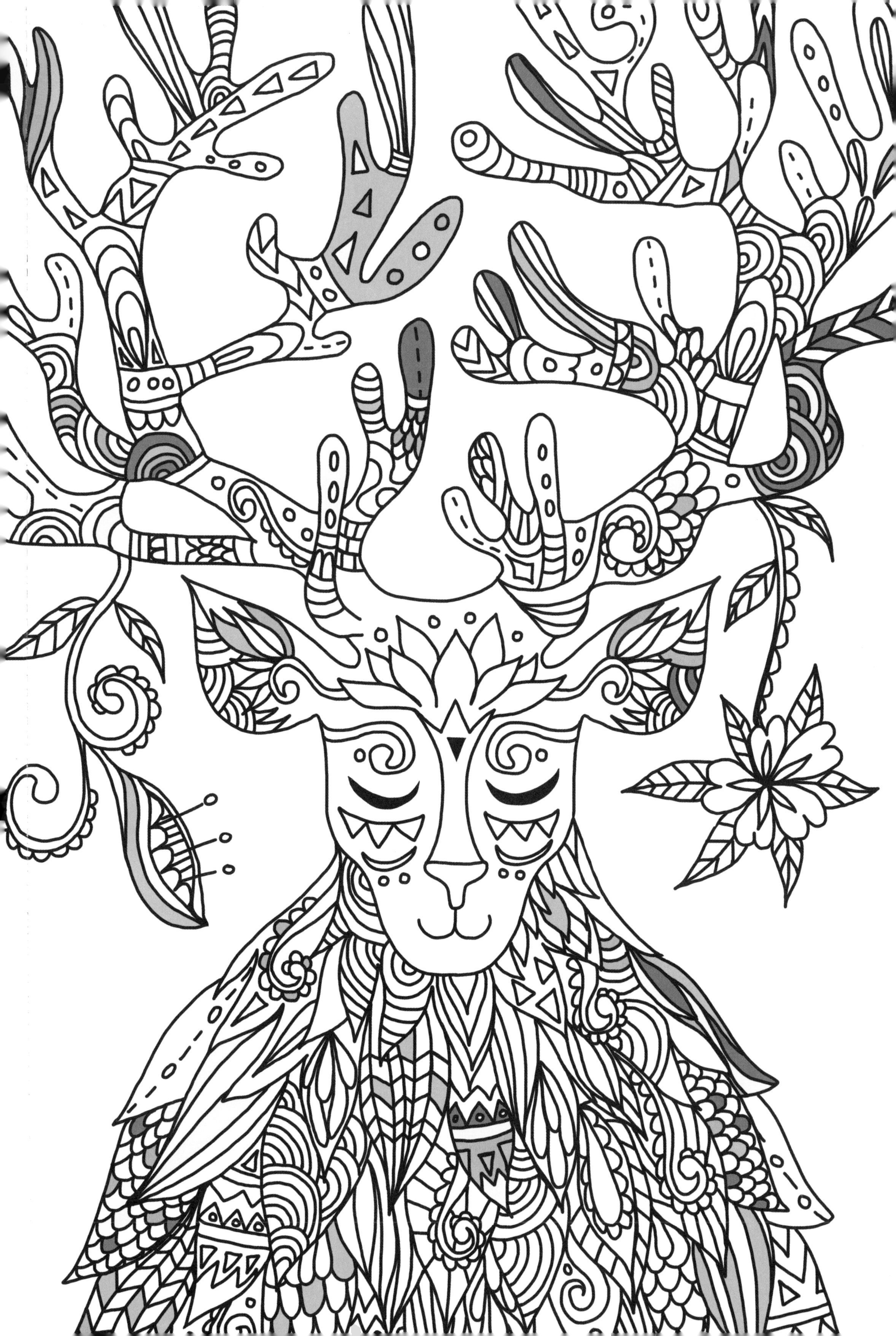

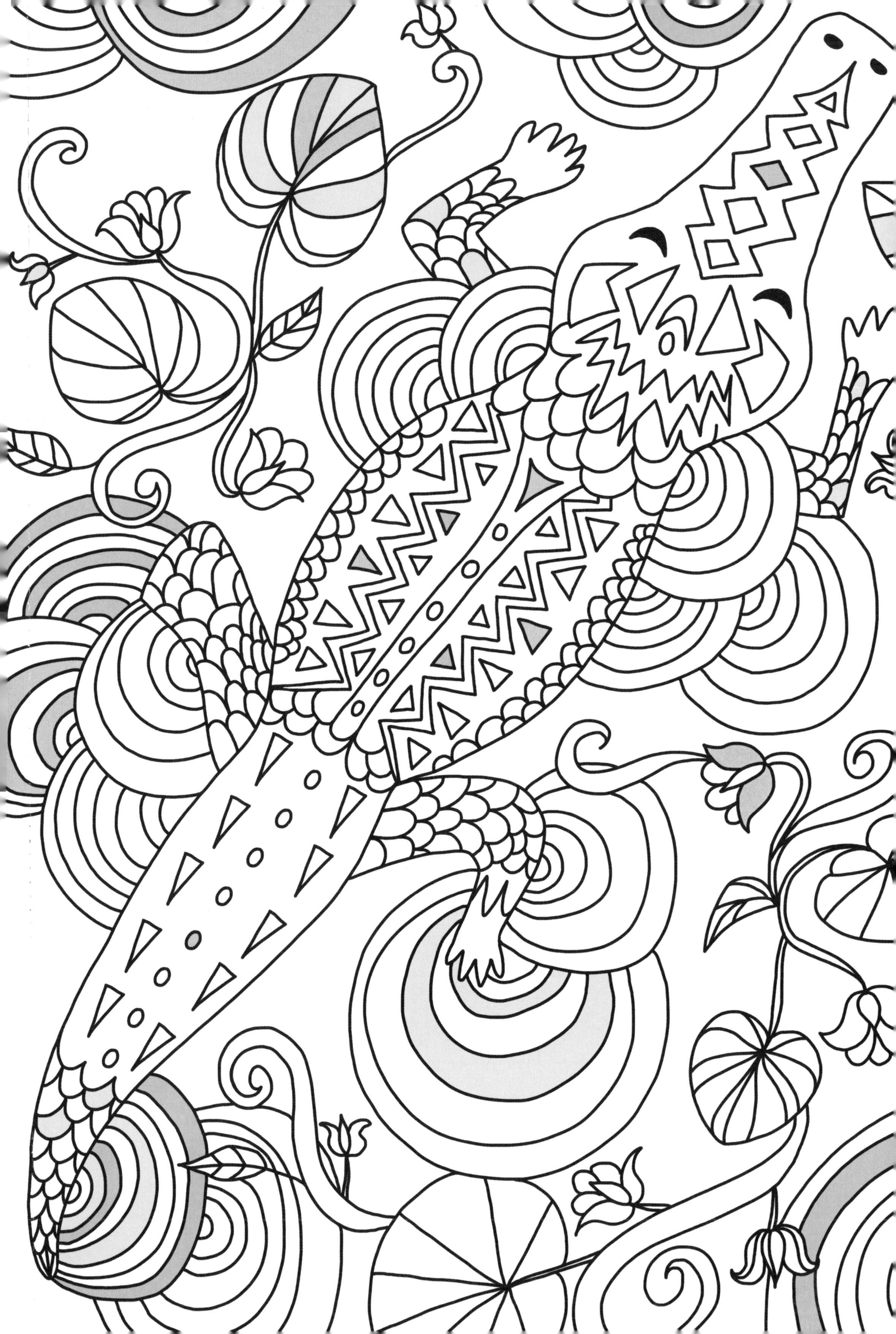

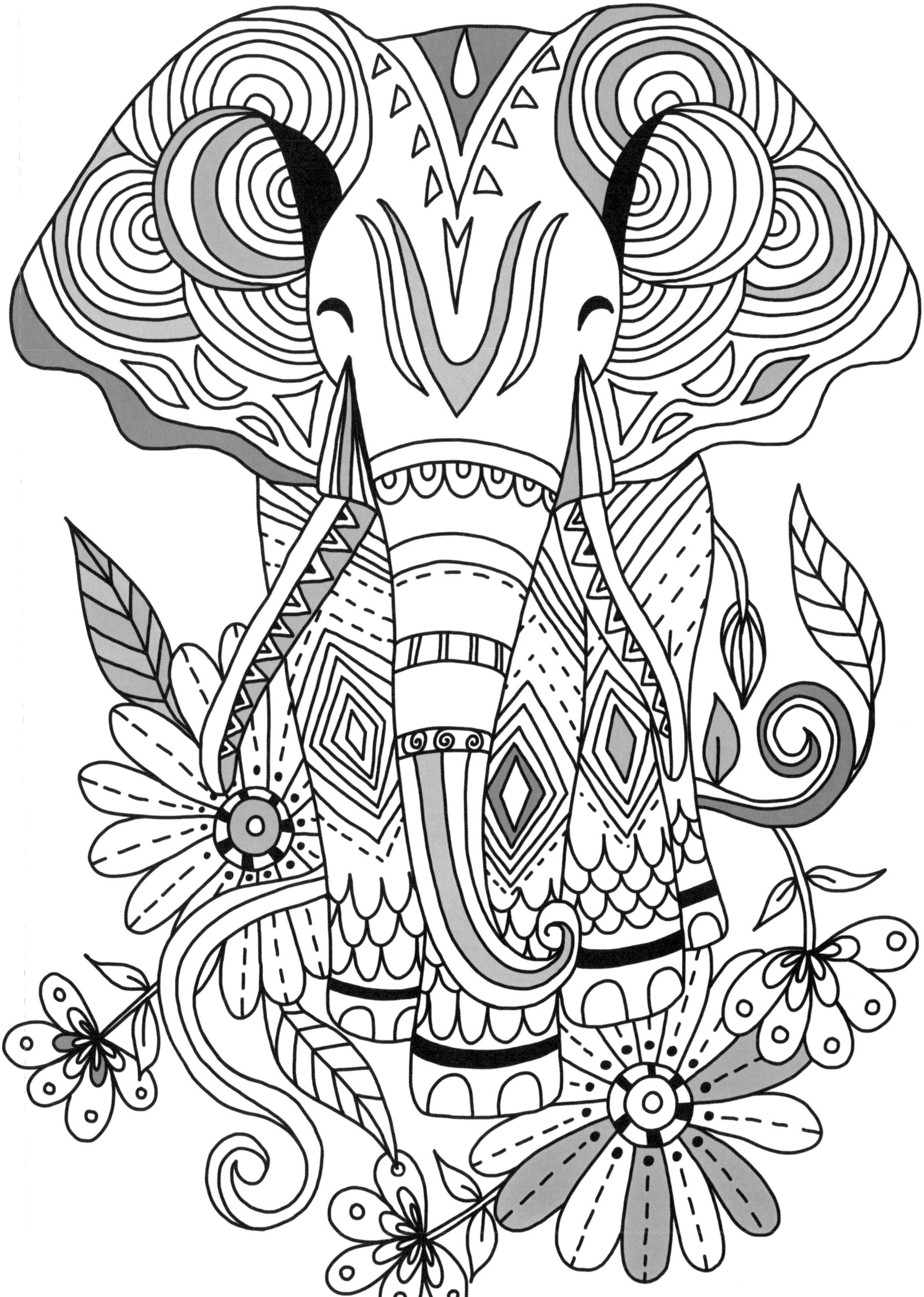

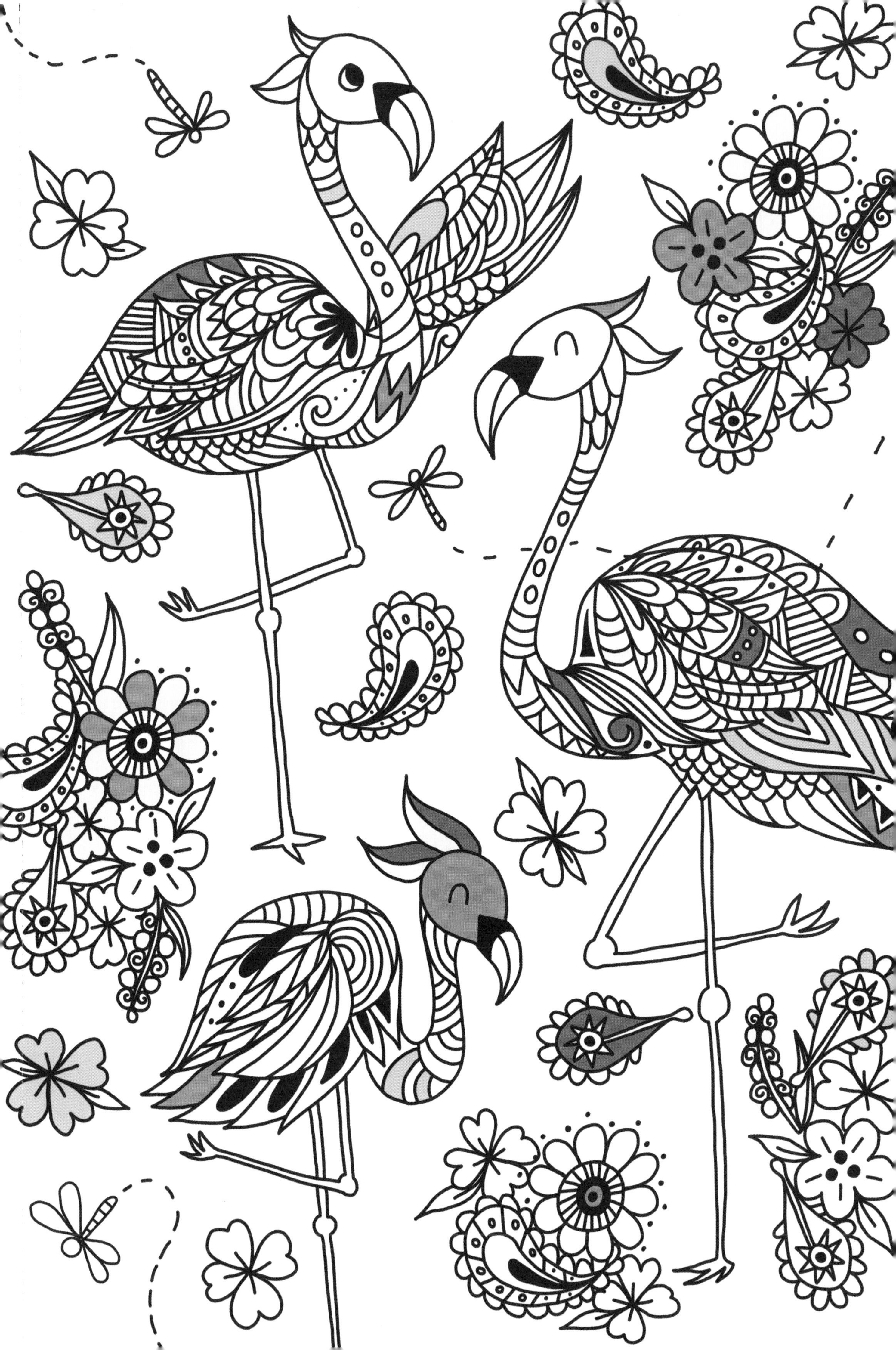

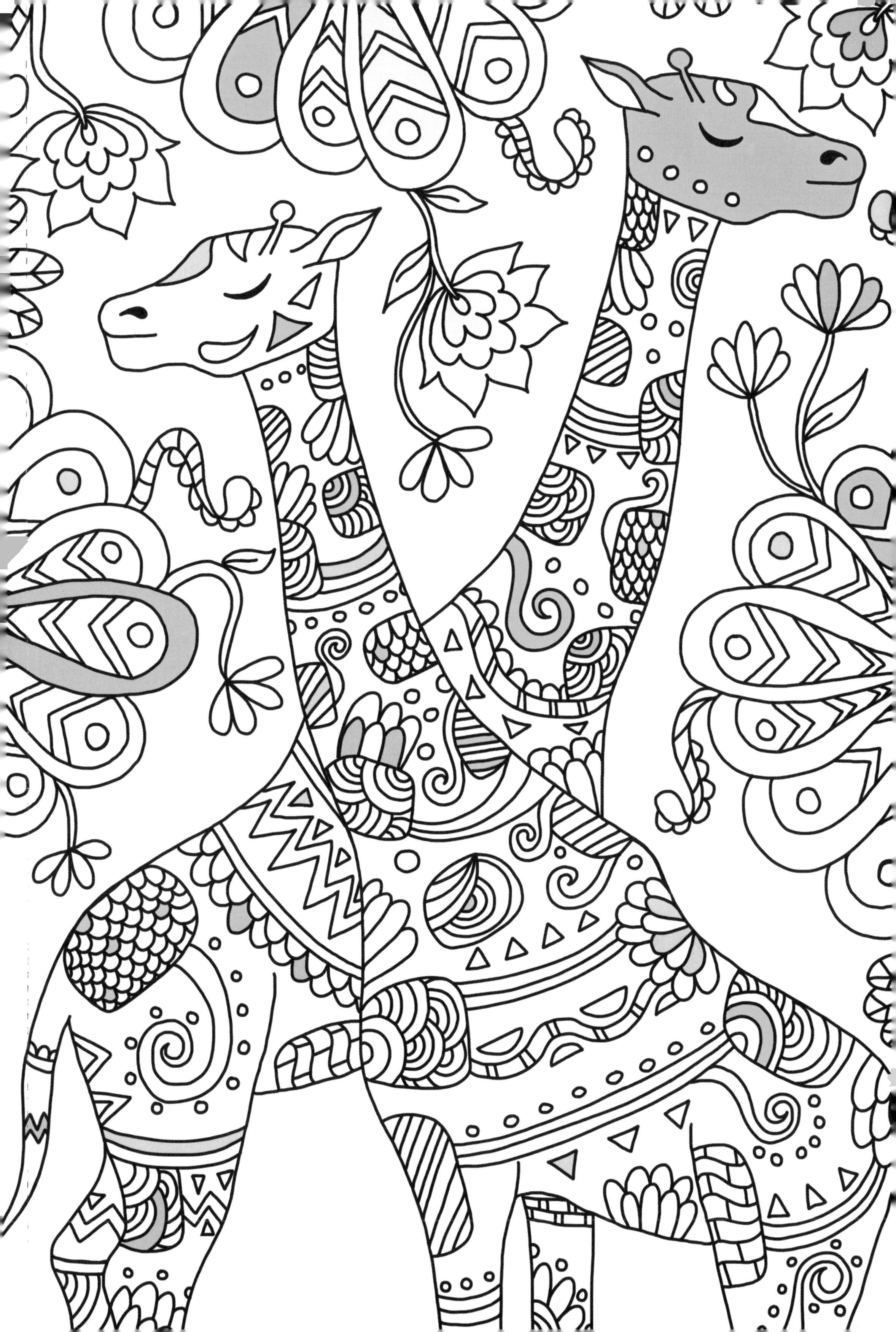

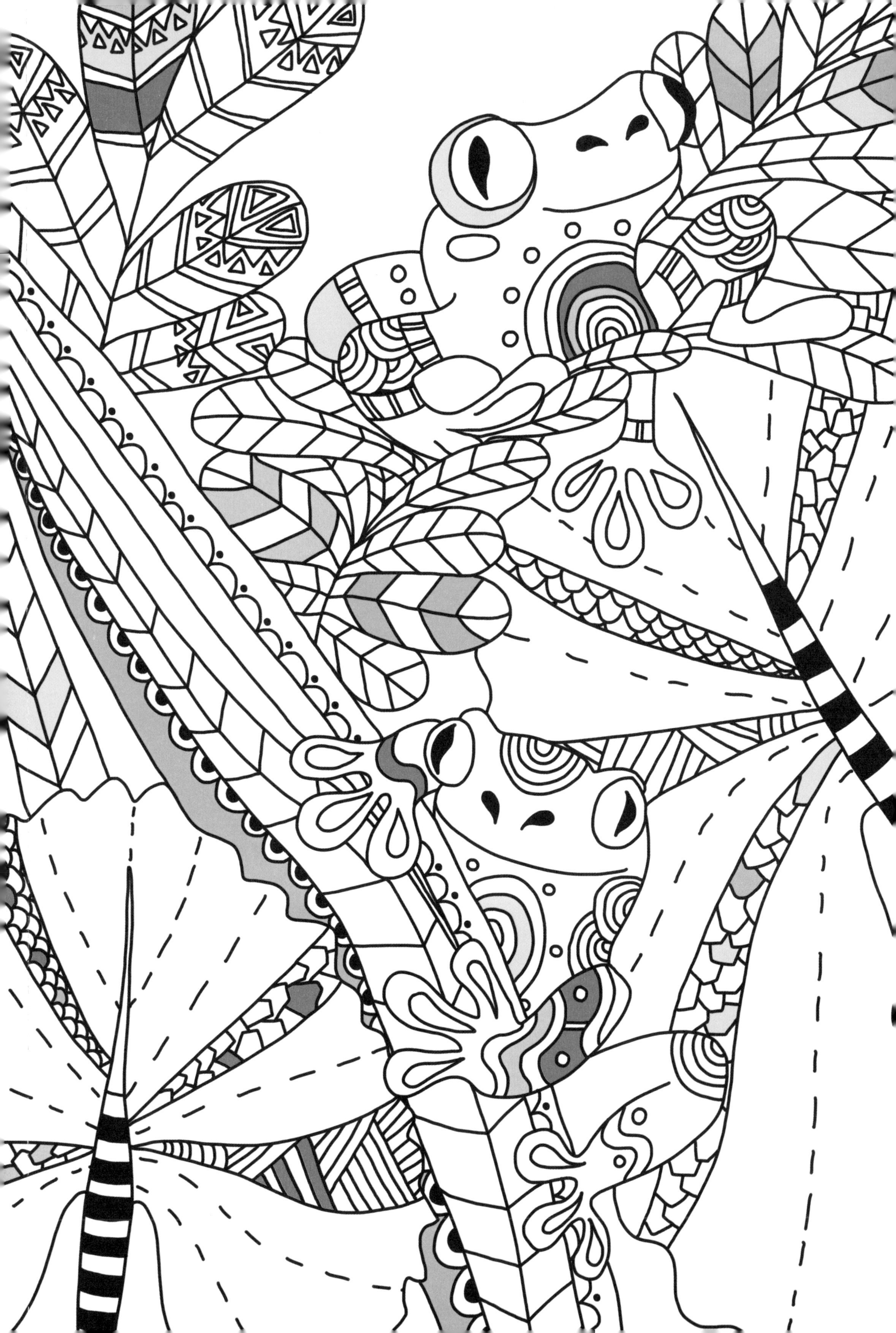

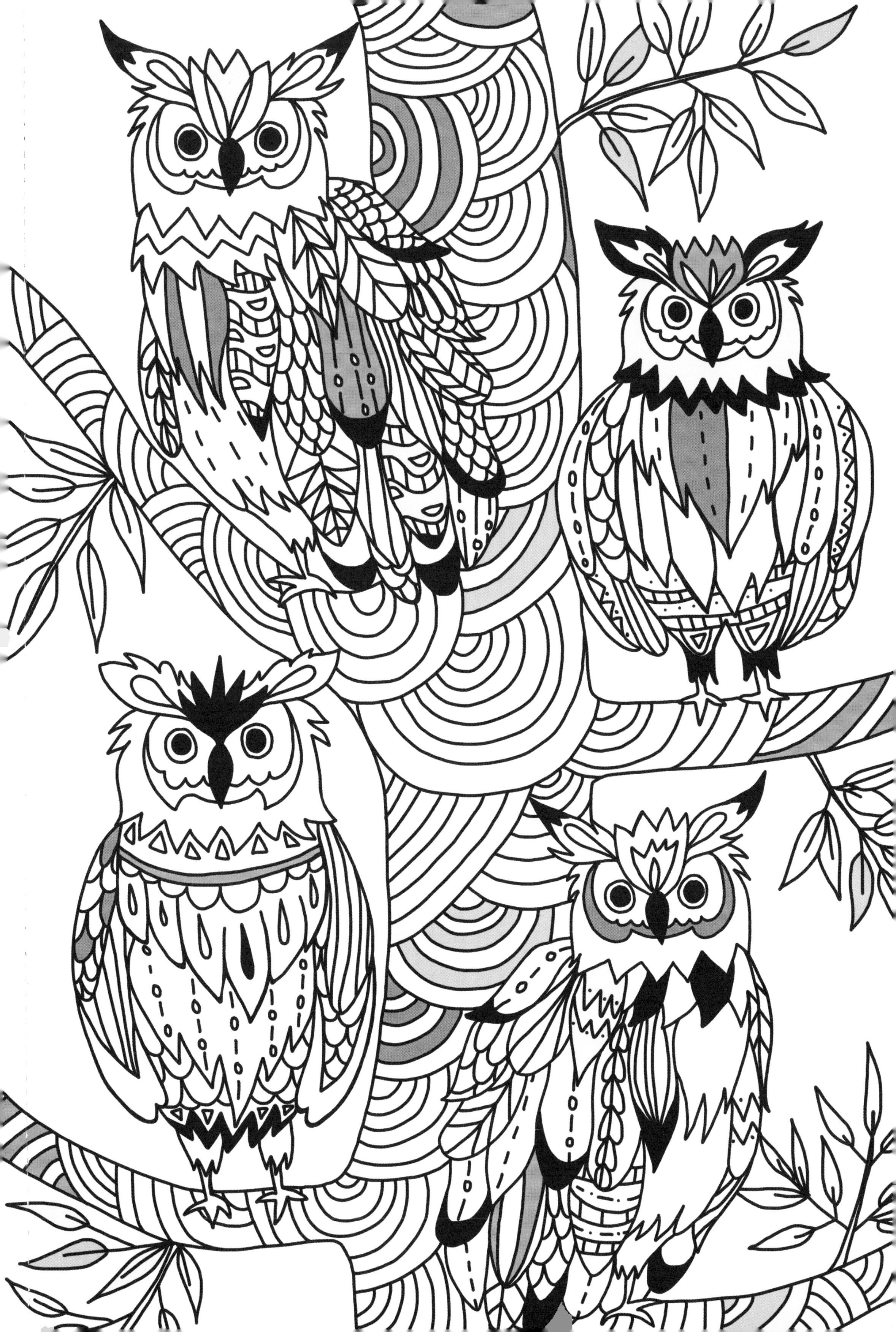

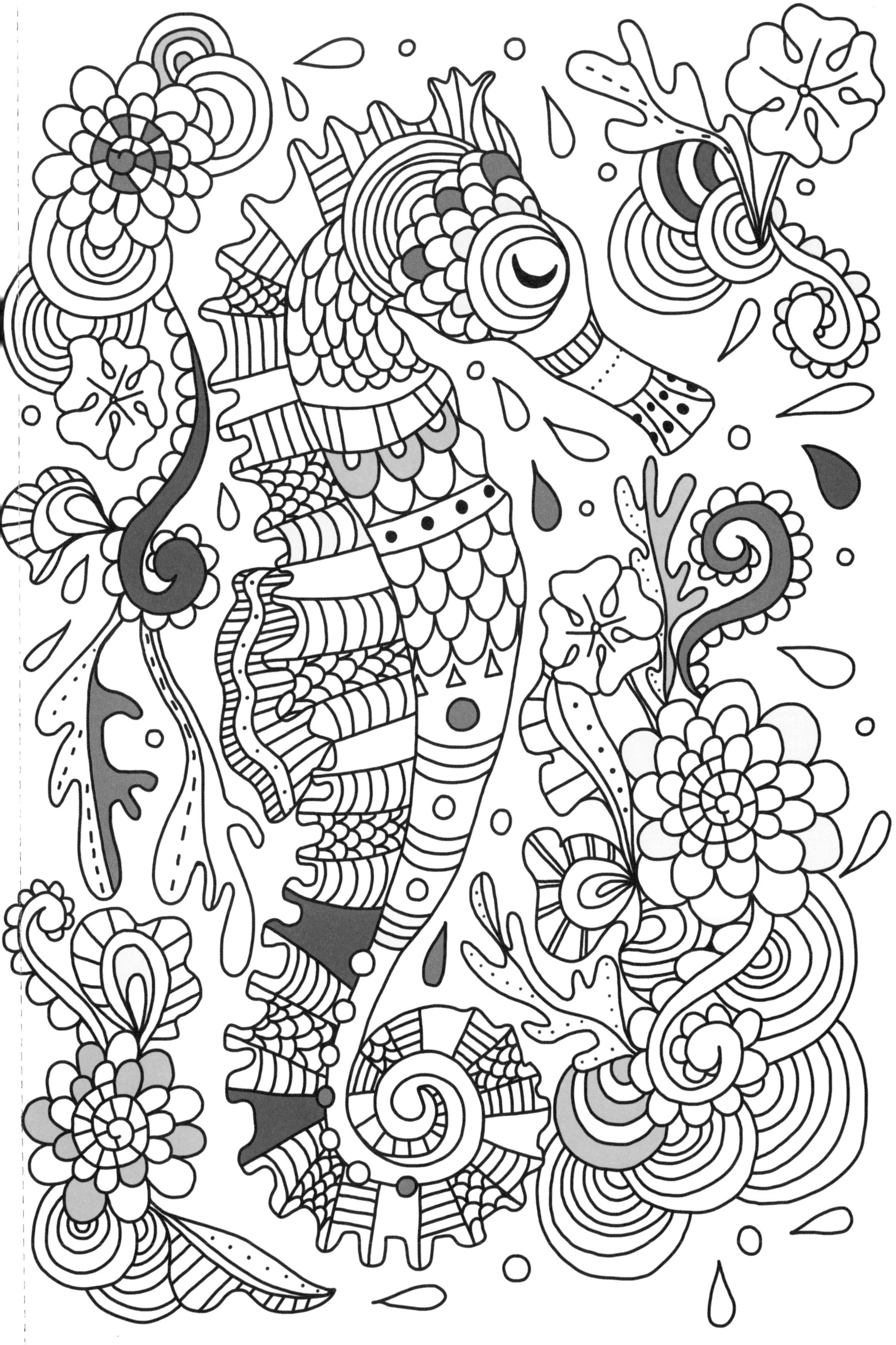

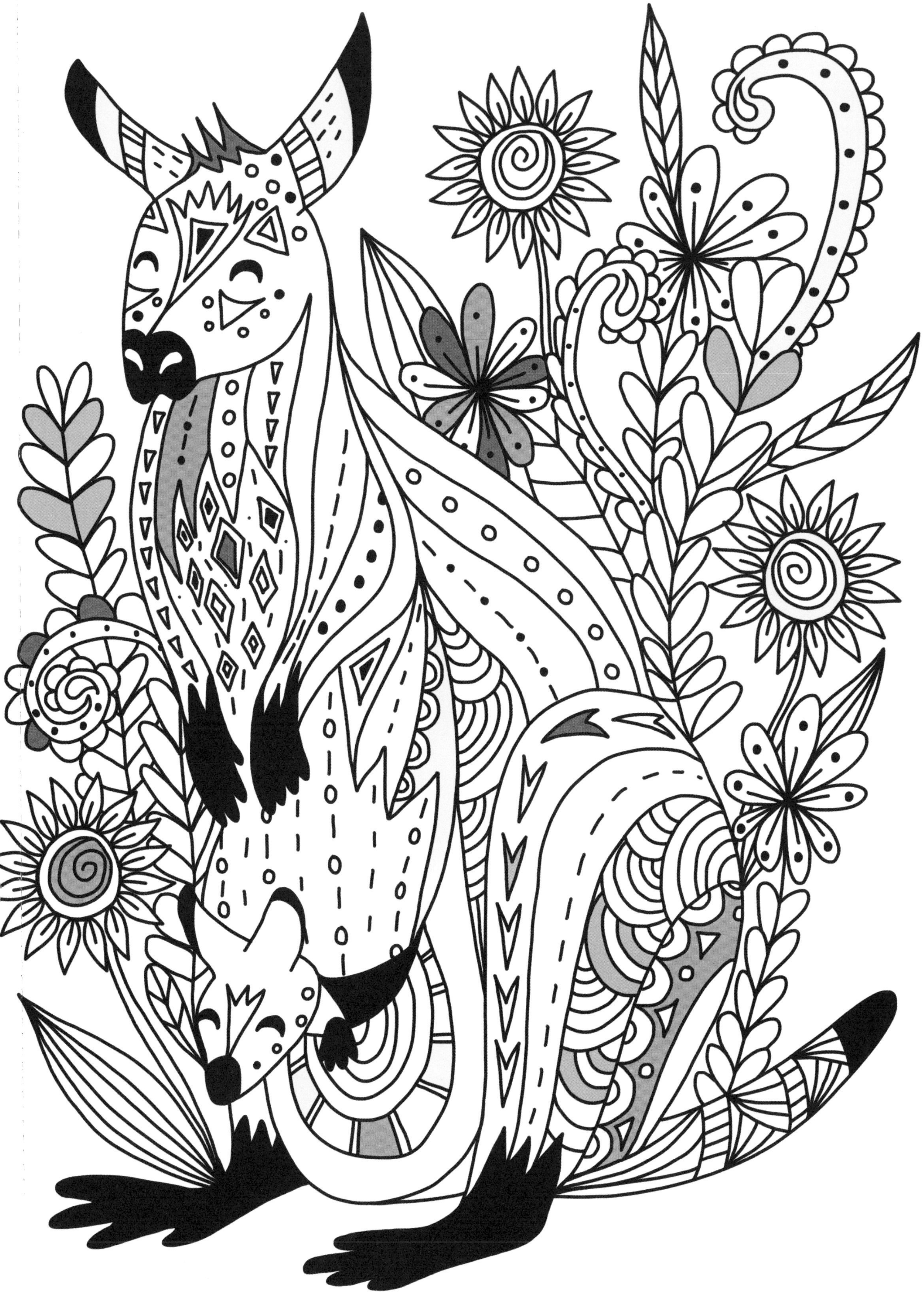

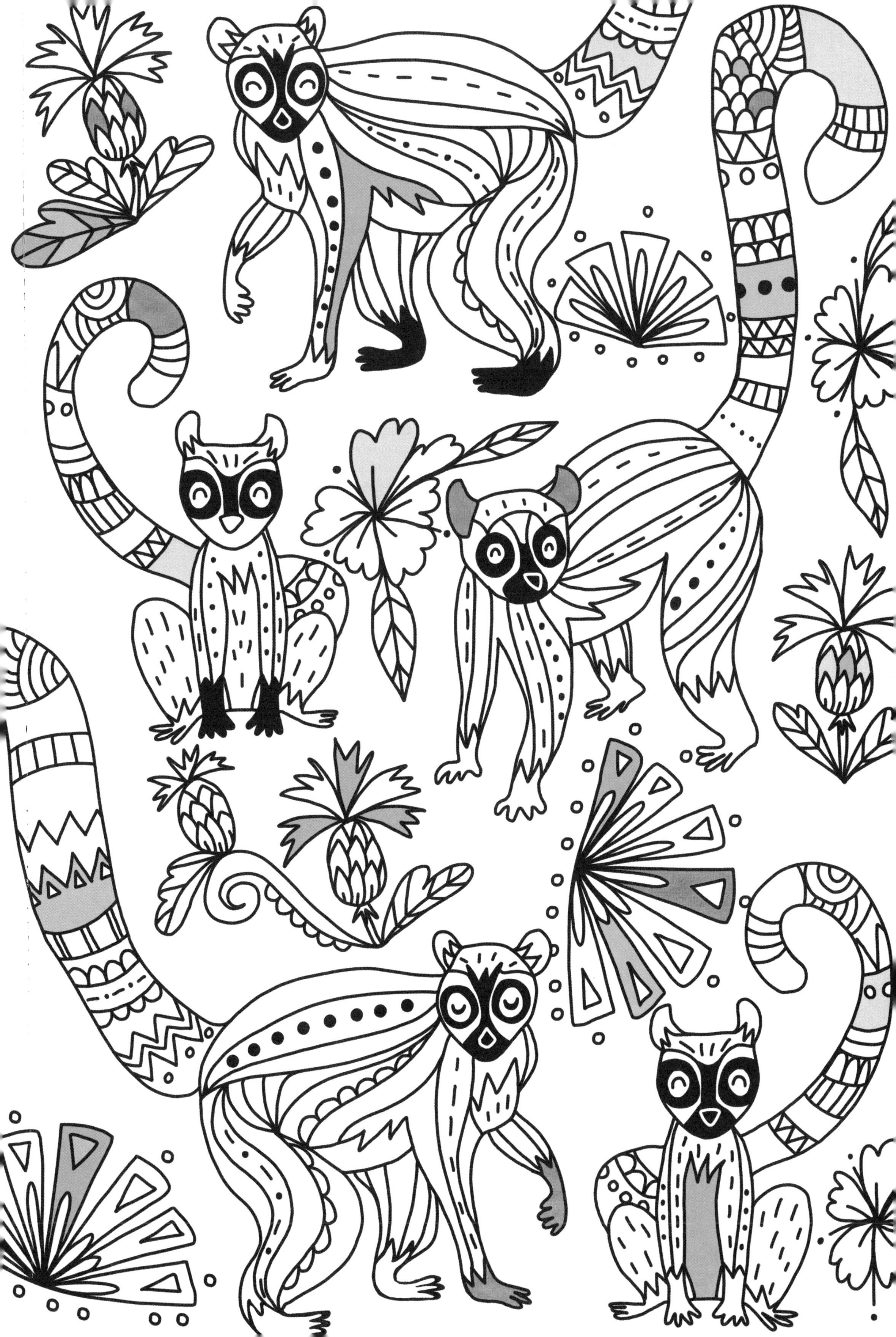

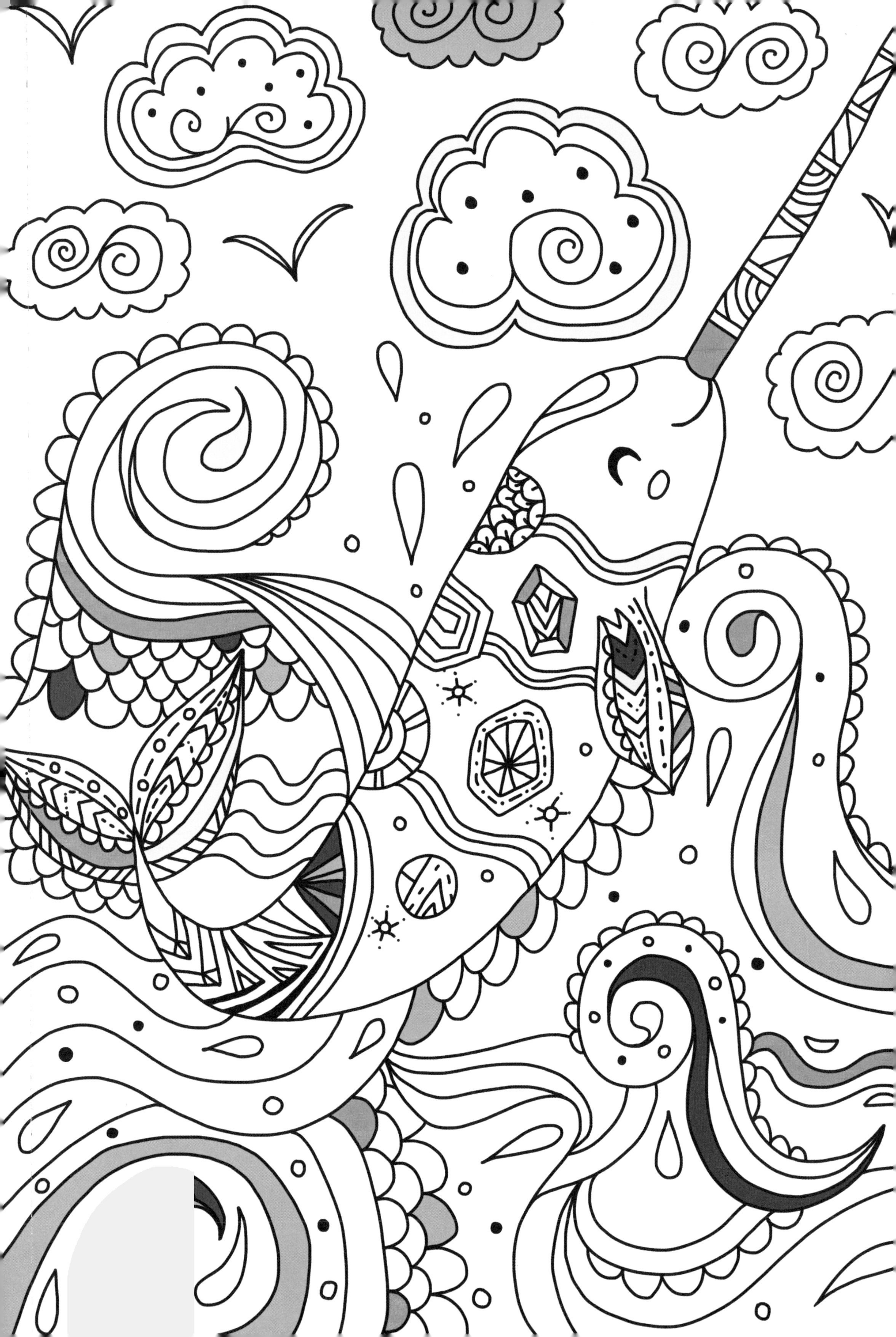

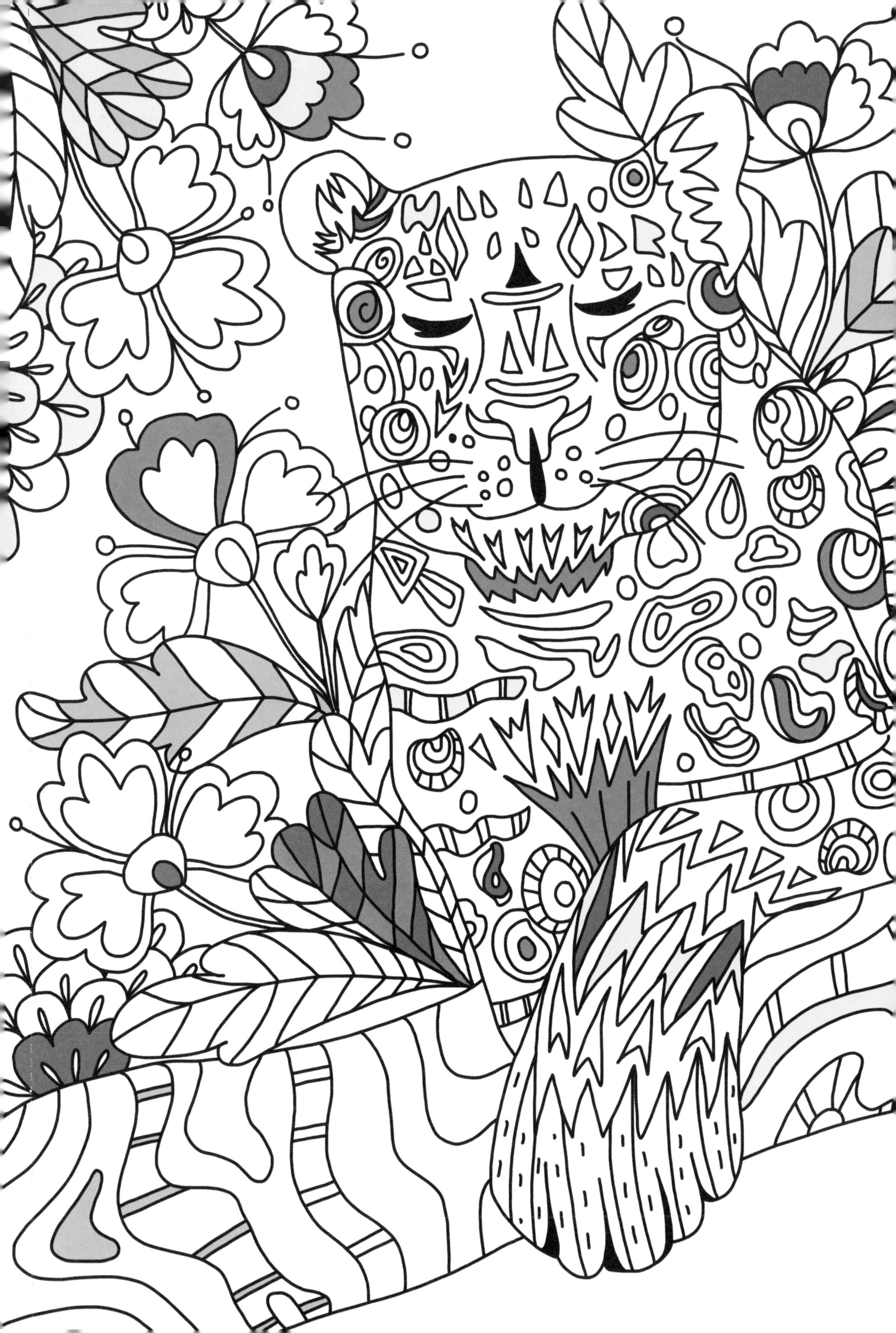

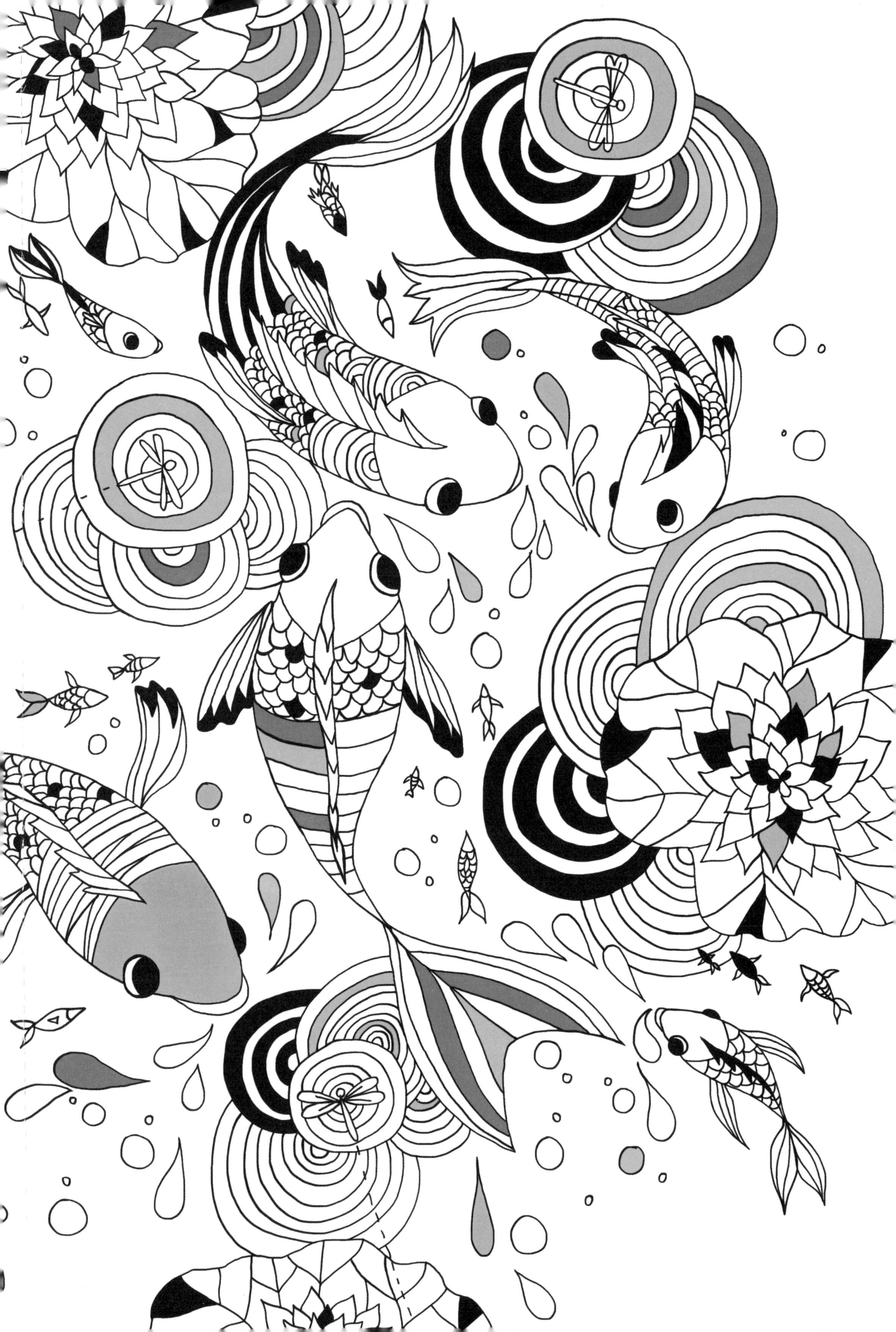

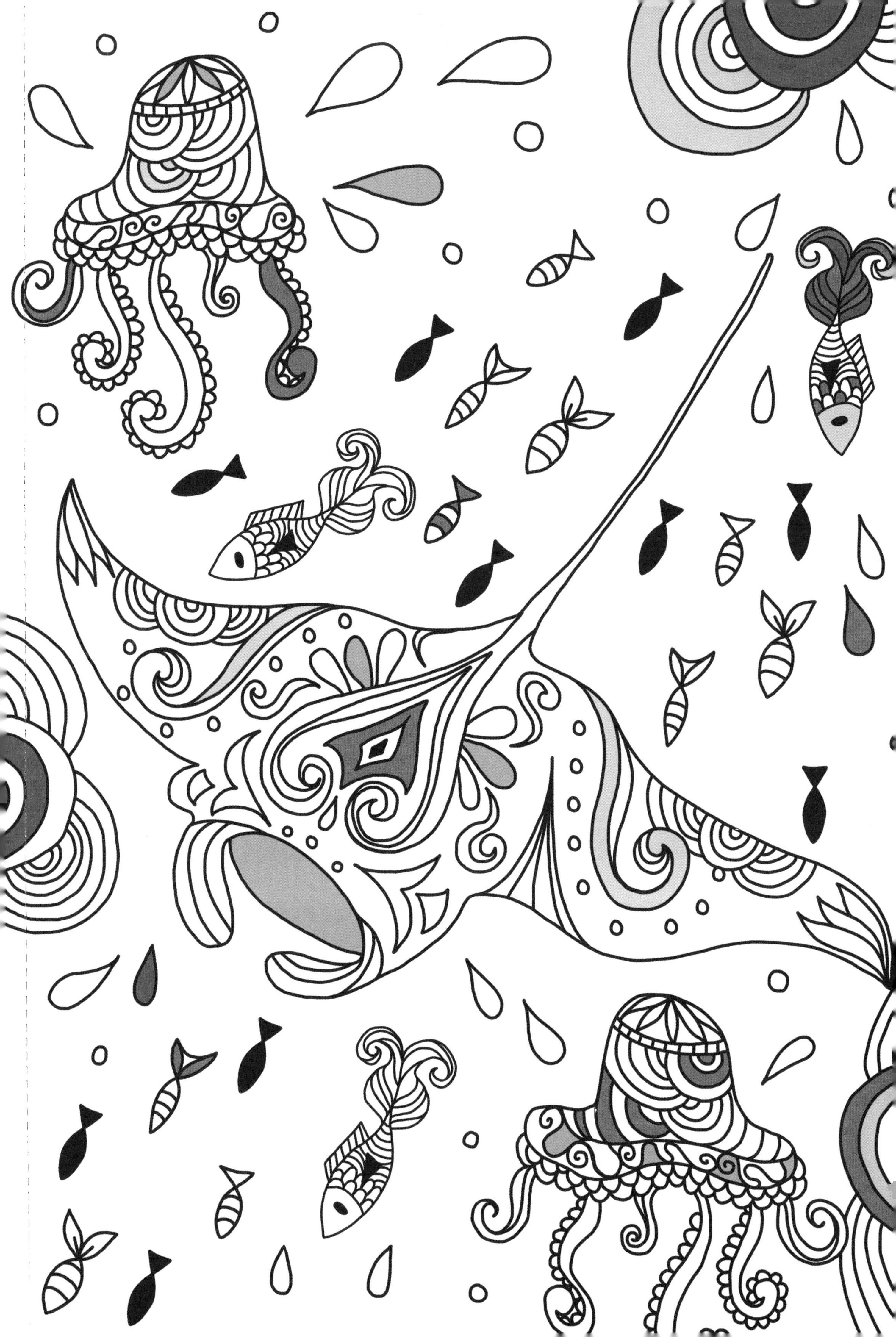

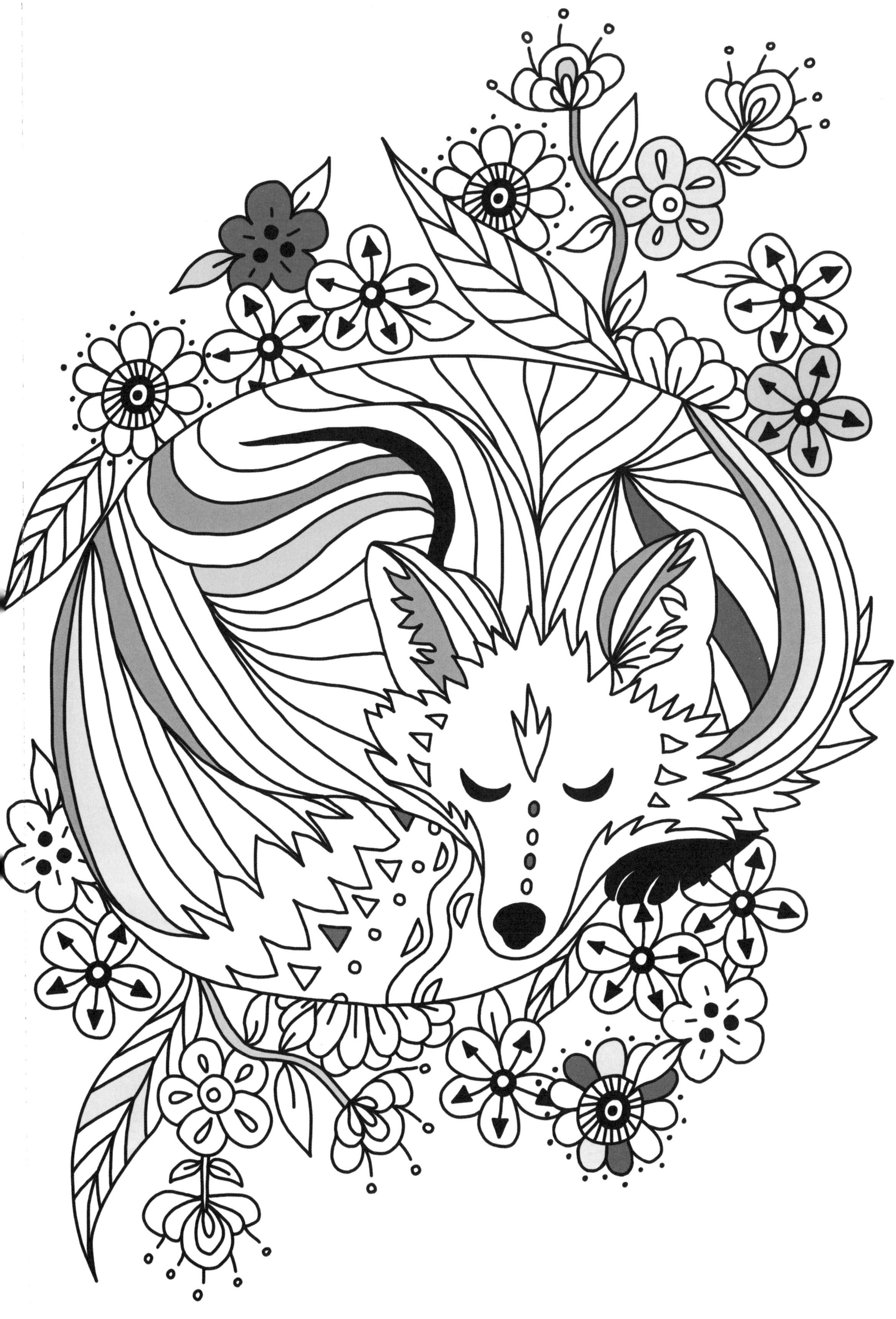

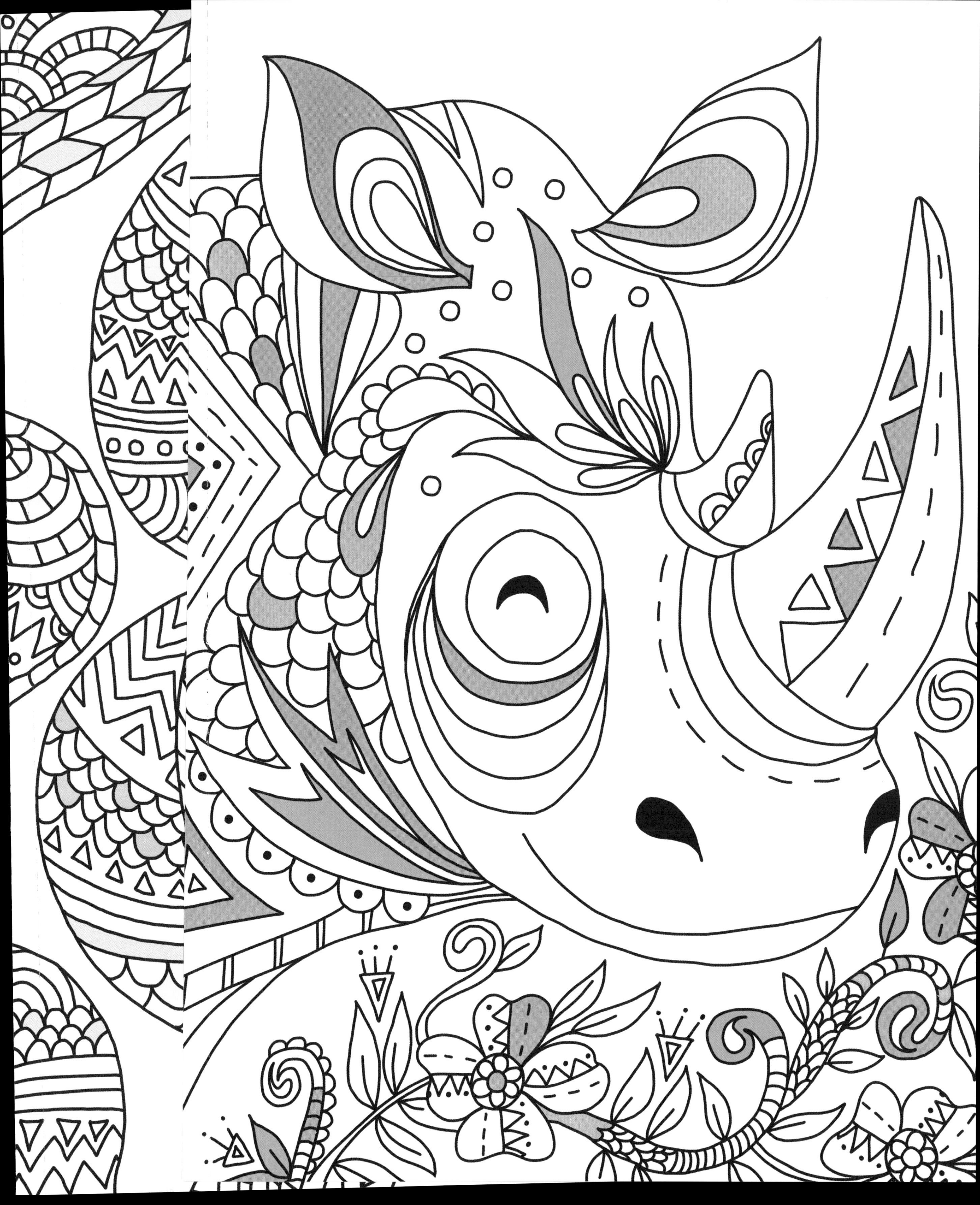

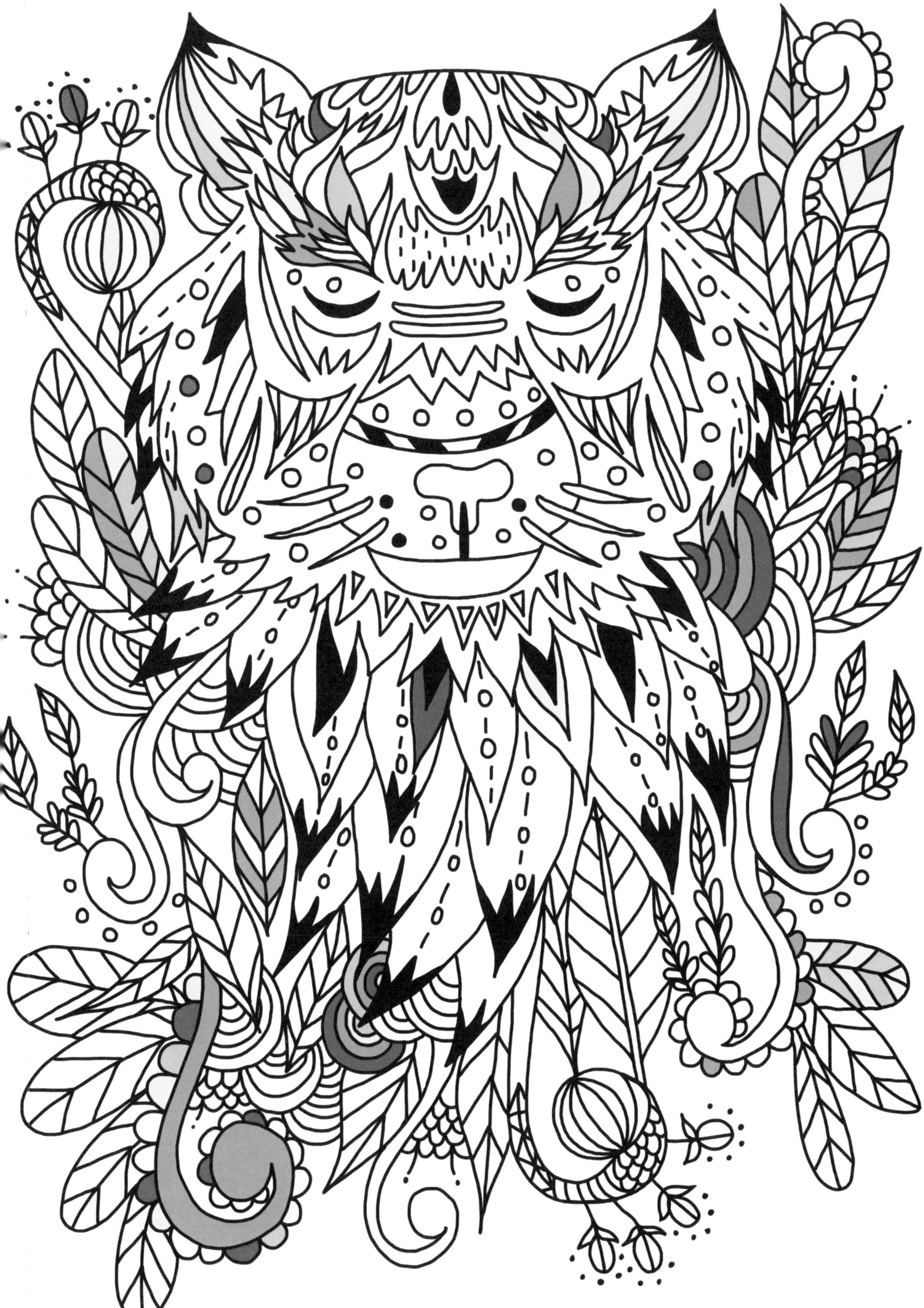

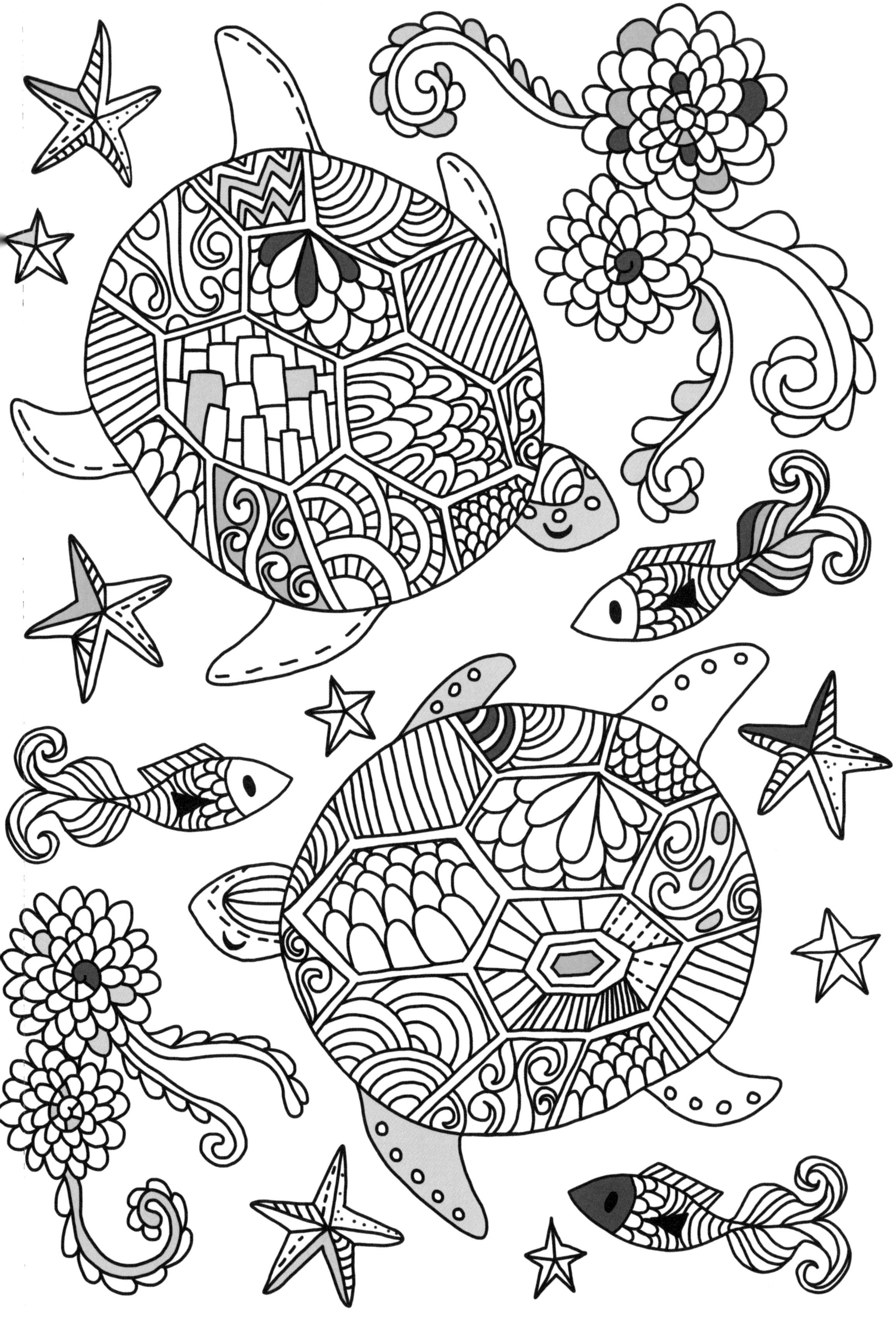

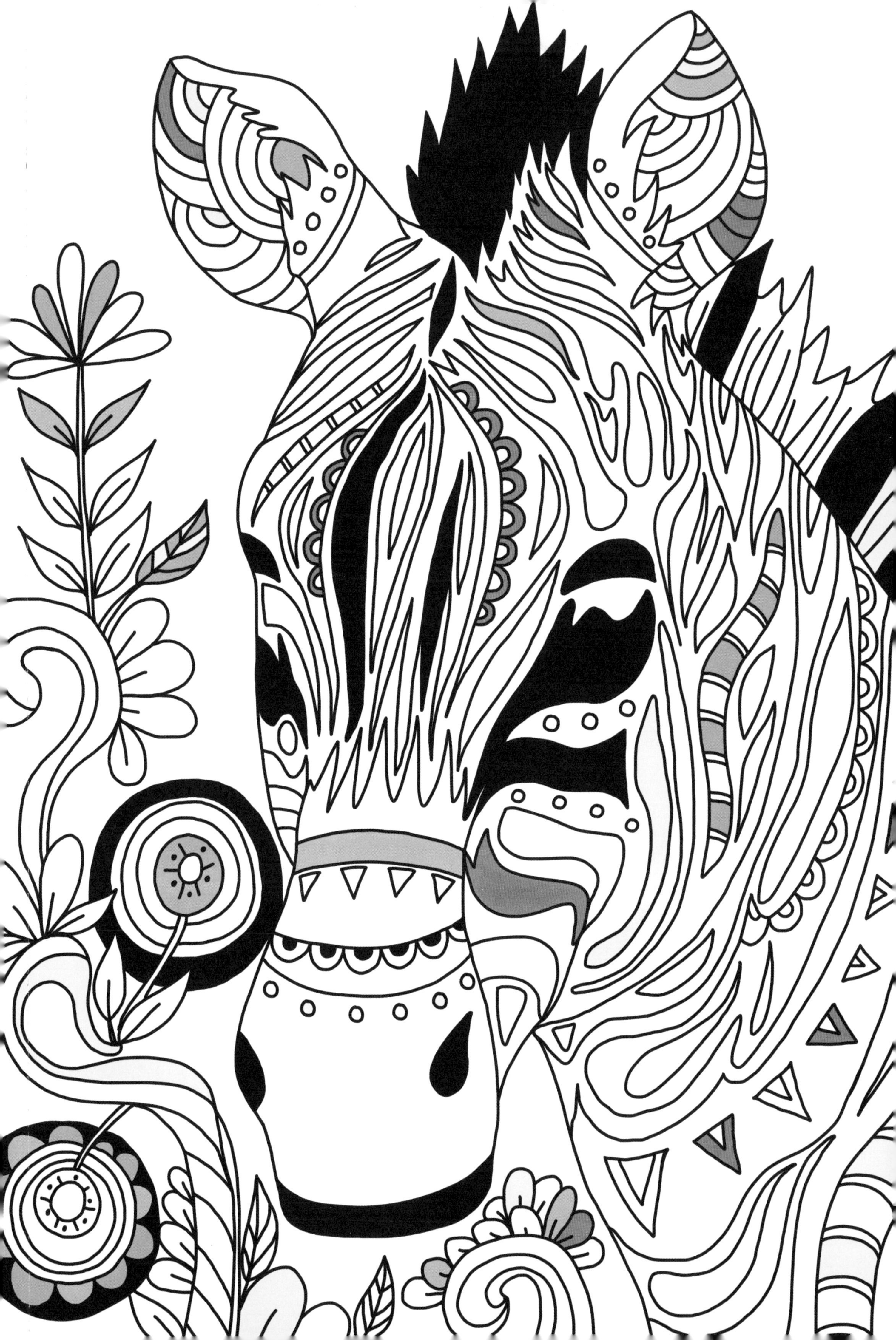